Jerusalem

The Jerusalem I love

*"Our feet have been standing
within your gates, O Jerusalem!
Peace be within your walls,
and security within your towers!"*
(Psalm 122:2, 7)

JOAN COMAY

THE JERUSALEM I LOVE

Photographer
DAVID HARRIS
General Editor
MORDECAI RAANAN

STEIMATZKY'S AGENCY
together with
NATEEV PUBLISHING

ACKNOWLEDGMENTS and thanks are due to the following persons for having kindly permitted the use of their photographs: Yael Braun—pages 20, 31, 45, 52, 53, 62, 66–67, 70, 76, 77, 84, 85, 87, 99, 102 (Upper right; lower left and right) 103, 105, 109, 112, 116–117, 121, 133, 136 (Upper right and left, lower right), 140 (Upper left), 146. Nuri Fisher—page 127.

Printed in Israel by Peli Printing Works Ltd.

BC	1000–961	(reign)	King David captures and makes Jerusalem the capital of the United Kingdom of Israel.
	961–922	(reign)	King Solomon builds the Temple.
	922		United Kingdom splits into Judah and Israel.
	715–687	(reign)	King Hezekiah of Judah builds tunnel from Gihon spring to bring water into the city, and strengthens the city walls.
	701		Jerusalem withstands the siege of Sennacherib, king of Assyria.
	587		Nebuchadnezzar, king of Babylon, conquers Jerusalem, destroys the Temple and exiles Jews to Babylonia.
	538		Cyrus, king of Persia, after conquering Babylon, allows Jewish exiles to return and build their Temple anew.
	515		Jews complete the reconstruction of the Temple known henceforth as the Second Temple.
	445–425		Nehemiah rebuilds the walls of Jerusalem.
	332		Beginning of Hellenistic period when Alexander the Great of Macedonia conquers the Persians.
	312–198		Jerusalem under the Ptolemies.
	198–167		Jerusalem under the Seleucids.
	169		Antiochus IV Epiphenes plunders the Temple.
	167–63		Mattathias (of the House of Hasmon) and his five sons launch the Maccabee revolt, recapture the Temple Mount, purify and re-dedicate the Temple in 164 BC, and inaugurate a century of Jewish independence under the Hasmoneans.
	63		The Roman general Pompey conquers Jerusalem and destroys the Temple.
	40–37		Brief re-establishment of Hasmonean rule.
	37–4	(reign)	Herod the Great.
	20		Herod starts rebuilding the Temple.

AD	6	Judea under Roman rule.
	(c.30)	Death of Jesus in Jerusalem.
	66–70	The Jewish war against the Romans.
	70	Sacking of Jerusalem and the destruction of the Temple by Titus.
	132–135	Bar Kochba's war of freedom—Jerusalem again the capital.
	135	Total destruction of Jerusalem by the Romans who then build on its ruins a new city called Aelia Capitolina; Jews are banned from the city.
	326	Emperor Constantine declares Christianity state religion and builds the Church of the Holy Sepulchre.
	614	Persian conquest of Jerusalem.
	629	Recaptured briefly by the Christians.
	638	Moslem conquest; Caliph Omar enters Jerusalem.
	691	Dome of the Rock completed.
	1099	Crusaders capture Jerusalem; Jews and Moslems banned.
	1187	Saladin captures Jerusalem from the Crusaders, returns Jerusalem. to Moslem rule.
	1538–1540	Sultan Suleiman rebuilds the walls of the city.
	1860	First Jewish settlement outside the city walls.
	1917	British conquest; General Allenby enters Jerusalem.
	1922	British mandate commences.
	1948	British mandate ends and State of Israel proclaimed.
	1948–1949	Israel's War of Independence.
	1949	Israel—Transjordan armistice agreement signed in which Jerusalem divided between the two countries. Jerusalem declared the capital of Israel.
	1967	Six Day War in which Israeli troops capture the Old City. Jerusalem liberated and re-united. All three faiths now have access to their Holy Places.

ILLUSTRATIONS

On entering the city for the first time, one feels the emotional impact of 4,000 years of continuous history, which have given the very word Jerusalem a profoundly mystic sound to hundreds of millions of Christians, Jews, and Moslems throughout the world. This is the city of David and Solomon, of Isaiah and Jeremiah, of Ezra and Nehemia, of Judas Maccabeus and his brothers. This is the city of Jesus' last ministry and the Crucifixion. And Moslems held this city to be the place from where Mohammed is believed to have ascended to Heaven.

It seems as if there has always existed a Jerusalem cradled in this high amphitheater, withdrawn from the busy traffic of the coastal plain and the desert routes—close to eternal things as it contemplated the rugged landscape and breathed in the pure mountain air.

Nothing about the serene air of Jerusalem today recalls its thirty-three centuries of turbulent history, including earthquakes, nineteen military sieges, two total destructions by conquerors, and many rebuildings. The existence and stubborn survival of an important city at this spot defies reason. It is far from the sea-coast or from any river basin, and off the important caravan routes of early times. Surrounded by bleak hills, it is difficult of access, and in past ages had scanty water sources—a single natural spring below the eastern wall, and underground cisterns hewn out of the rock to hold rainwater.

However, its position on the great divide between the coastal plain and the Jordan valley, and at the heart of the highlands of Judah and Samaria, has always given Jerusalem a strategic value. But it was the Hebrew kings and above all the Hebrew prophets who gave it greatness.

Its beginnings are lost in the mists of anti-

Jerusalem under the summer sun and winter clouds. The view, right, is taken from the ridge of the Mount of Olives, the one below from its western slope, and it epitomizes the meaning of Jerusalem to three religious faiths: the window of a Christian chapel above the Garden of Gethsemane looks out upon the Moslem Dome of the Rock and the Mosque of El-Aksa, sited on the sacred Jewish Temple Mount where king Solomon built the House of the Lord some three thousand years ago. Beneath the snow in the foreground (right) lie the graves of Jews from many centuries and many countries who were laid to rest within sight of the Temple compound in the most ancient and revered Jewish cemetery in the world. In the distance rise the structures of the New City, vibrant with life.

"Thy lightnings lit up the world". (Psalms, 77:19)

quity. It is already there when Abraham the Patriarch arrives in the Promised Land and accepts "bread and wine" from its Canaanite king, Melchi-zedek. Centuries later, when Joshua invades the country through Jericho, it is Jerusalem's Adoni-zedek who forms a coalition of five Canaanite rulers to block his advance.

The word "zedek" (righteousness)—as part of the names of these two Jerusalem kings—suggests the early religious significance of the city.

Since Jewish settlement in their Promised Land, how often has Jerusalem been pagan, Christian or Moslem? How many different conquerors have wielded their power over it: Jebusites, Egyptians, Babylonians, and Persians; Greeks and Romans; Moslem Arabs, Seljuks, Fatimids, Crusaders, Mamelukes, Ottomans, and British. At times, its buildings burgeoned into splendor, under King Solomon, Herod the Great, the Emperor Constantine, and Sultan Suleiman the Magnificent. At other times, it was reduced to rubble, with the blood of the slaughtered citizens flowing down its gutters.

But throughout the flux of these thousands of years there runs one constant thread—the unique attachment of the Jewish people to Jerusalem. This attachment has remained unbroken from the time when King David made Jerusalem the capital of Israel to the time when David Ben-Gurion did so 3,000 years later. Through all the centuries of dispersion, in the farthest corners of the earth, Jews have prayed for the return to Zion—as Jerusalem is often called in the Bible—and built their synagogues with the Sacred Ark pointing in the direction where the Temple of Solomon once stood. History has no parallel to this mystic bond, and without it there would have been no State of Israel.

Jews at prayer at the Western ("Wailing") Wall on the Festival of Succot (below), bearing the traditional *lulav* (palm frond) and *etrog* (citron) and (right) beginning to gather before this hallowed site on the eve of Israel's Independence Day anniversary celebrations. The Wall, part of king Herod's construction in the 1st century BC, is the sole relic of the Temple compound to survive the Roman destruction in 70 AD, and it has been revered ever since by Jews throughout the world as their most sacred Holy Place. The term "Wailing Wall", applied by the Gentiles, is believed to stem from the 4th century when the Roman prohibition on Jewish entry into Jerusalem was lifted for one day in the year to enable Jews to come and "wail over its ruins". In ancient times, it was to the Temple of Jerusalem that the "congregation of Israel" thronged to celebrate the three religious pilgrim festivals of Passover, Pentecost and Succot. With the re-unification of Jerusalem after the 1967 Six Day War, Jews once again can fulfil the biblical injunction of festival pilgrimage, and enjoy free access at all times to their most sacred shrine.

Singly or in groups, on weekday, Sabbath and Festival, at all times of the day and night throughout the year, Jews from all parts of Israel and from many lands overseas come to pray or pay silent homage at the Western Wall of the Temple compound. The shadow in the picture (left), cast by the ornamental detail in the chain along the forecourt (seen in top right), is reminiscent of the ritual seven-branched *menorah* (candelabrum) which stood in the Temple, and which is today the symbol of the State of Israel.

The golden Dome of the Rock, or Mosque of the Dome (preceding page). Erected on the ruined site of the Jewish Temple compound some fifty years after the Moslem conquest in the 7th century AD—seventeen centuries after the building of Solomon's Temple—it underwent considerable repair and received numerous decorative additions in the years that followed. But this magnificent octagonal structure is substantially the same today as it was when completed in the year 691.

Erroneously ascribed to the earlier Caliph Omar, and therefore often called the Mosque of Omar, it was in fact built by the Caliph Abd el-Malik, as much for political and economic as for religious reasons. He sought to divert Moslem pilgrimage from Mecca with whose caliph he was in fierce conflict. The site he chose was the sacred altar-rock of the Jewish Temple in Jerusalem—for that was interpreted as having been the rock which figured in a dream by Mohammed while sojourning in his cave-retreat in Arabia. In the dream, Mohammed, accompanied by an angel, rode through the skies on the back of his steed from distant Arabia to Jerusalem's Temple rock, and was caught up through the seven heavens into the presence of Allah. The gilded dome was erected directly above the rock.

The Dome of the Rock stands on the highest point of the Jewish Temple compound, which was re-named Haram esh-Sharif, "Noble Sanctuary", by the Arabs. At its southern end, the silver-domed mosque of El-Aksa was erected by Abd el-Malik's son early in the 8th century, but little of the original structure remains. The present building is the product of subsequent reconstructions by Moslem rulers in later centuries, who also beautified the Haram esh-Sharif with gates, minarets, arcades, and fountains like the one (below) in the plaza in front El-Aksa, to serve the Moslem worshippers (right) on festive occasions.

One of the ornate entrances (left) to the Dome of the Rock. The strip running across the top of the exquisitely tiled surface, above the arch, bears verses from the Koran in elaborate Arabic script. Below, the interior of the sanctuary, the Rock encircled by columns which support the Dome.

DAVID'S JERUSALEM

It was the redoutable King David (1000–961 BC)—warrior, statesman and poet—who indelibly linked Jerusalem for all time to the Jewish religion, nation and state. David had been King Saul's son-in-law and favorite until he incurred the monarch's jealousy, and had to flee to the precarious existence of an outlaw. On Saul's death in battle against the Philistines, David became king of the southern area settled by his native tribe of Judah, with his capital at Hebron. After two years of confused struggle, David was accepted as their ruler by the northern Israelite tribes as well. Reigning over a united kingdom, David would complete the process of uniting the tribes begun by Saul, destroy the Philistine threat, and bring security to the country.

But at the very outset, while David was still headquartered in Hebron, he was faced with the existence of one hostile enclave inside Israelite territory, which had remained unsubdued during Joshua's campaign two hundred years earlier. This was the Jebusite stronghold of Jerusalem which lay like a dangerous wedge between the two portions of the kingdom. David took it by assault, promptly established himself there, and made it the capital of the country. It had the political advantage of not being located in the settled territory of any of the tribes, and so there could be no tribal jealousy. At the same time, it was fairly centrally situated between the northern and southern parts of the kingdom. And it was comparatively easy to defend, being built on the Ophel spur with deep valleys on three sides: Kidron to the east, Hinnom to the south, and the Central Valley to the west. Only from the north was it vulnerable.

It was to Jerusalem that David now brought the holiest object of the Hebrew faith, the Ark of the Covenant. It had rested at the

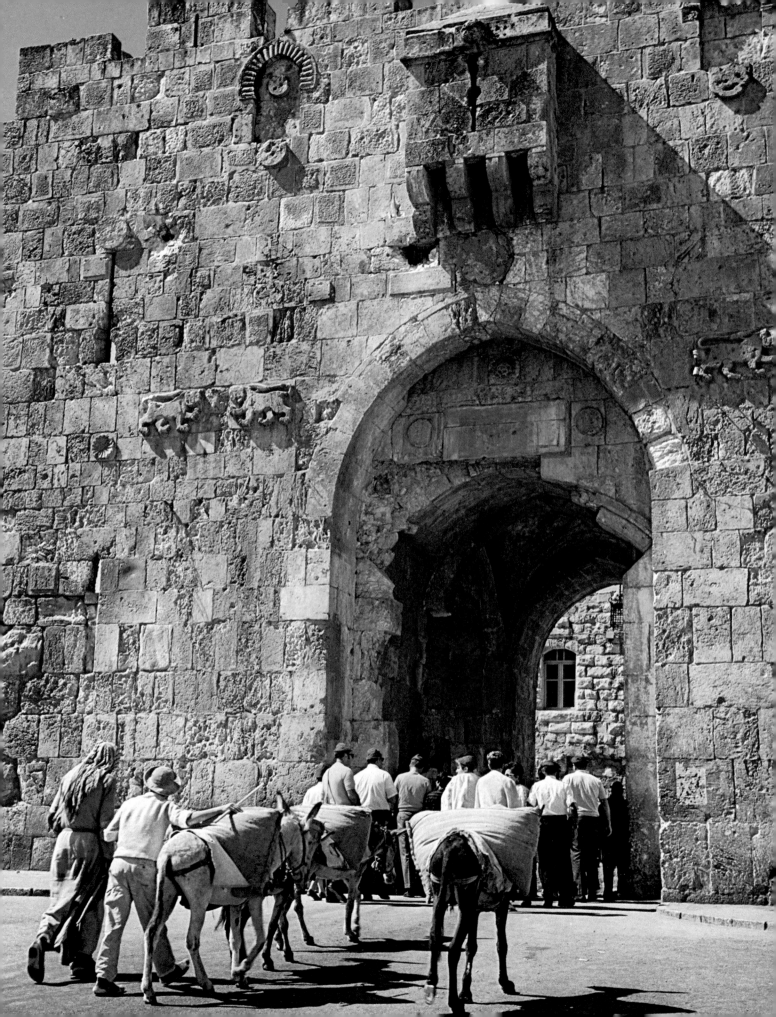

Passing the Citadel on their way to early morning Sabbath services, the Hassidim (below), just inside the Jaffa Gate, are making for the Western Wall. The nuns (right) are approaching the Gate to worship at the Holy Sepulchre in the Christian Quarter.

26

Damascus Gate (below), in the center of the Old City's northern wall, is the most graceful of all the entrances, and was the prized structure of Suleiman the Magnificent, who towards the middle of the 16th century built the walls of the city which stand today. Archaeological excavations have brought to light remains of the 2nd century Roman gate on this site (bottom left). Suleiman's Damascus Gate, its arched portal set in a broad facade flanked on each side by a great tower and topped by battlements, is considered one of the richest examples of early Ottoman architecture in the region.

Dominating the Christian Quarter of the Old City (right) is the Basilica of the Holy Sepulchre, with its two cupolas (foreground). Built by the Emperor Constantine in the 4th century, it underwent frequent destruction and reconstruction in subsequent centuries. The larger of the two domes covers the rotunda, in the center of which lies the sepulchre itself.

The southern wing of the Citadel (left), the outstanding Jerusalem landmark adjoining Jaffa Gate, with Ottoman and Mameluke superstructures built on Crusader, Herodian and Hasmonean ruins. It was here that King Herod built his palace-fortress in the 1st century BC. Since Byzantine times the Citadel has also been known as the Tower of David—though it has no Davidic associations—and the name was later applied to the minaret alone. This minaret is a 17th century addition to a 14th century mosque. The view of it (right) is through a northern archway of the Citadel compound, across the court where archaeologists have exposed the remains of antiquity.

hilltop sanctuary of Kirjath-jearim, eight miles to the west of the city, since it had been recovered from the Philistines twenty years earlier. The Ark was installed in a large tent as its temporary home. By this act, Jerusalem became the religious as well as the political center of the kingdom. It did much to consolidate central authority.

The site for the future Temple was acquired by David when he bought the "threshing-floor of Araunah the Jebusite" for fifty shekels of silver, erected an altar on it and offered sacrifices. It lay on the highest point of the ridge immediately north of the Jebusite city which David had captured. Later tradition identified this hilltop with Mount Moriah, site of the dramatic episode of the sacrifice Abraham was called upon to make of his son Isaac.

David intended to build a Temple to the Lord on this spot as a permanent abode for the Ark. He said to the court prophet Nathan:

Part of the wall of the Old City which bounds the Citadel. Herod built well, and his palace became the subsequent citadel-residence of the Roman procurators, a stronghold of the Jewish resisters in the great battle for Jerusalem in 70 AD, the site of the Roman Legion camp thereafter, a headquarters of the Byzantines, the fortress of the Moslems, the castle of the Crusaders, and the Turkish citadel right up to Allenby's conquest in 1917. Today, preserved and restored, it houses a charming museum.

"See now, I dwell in a house of cedar, but the ark of God dwells in a tent" (2 Sam. 7:2). In the name of the Lord, Nathan vetoed the proposal. In the Book of Chronicles, it was suggested that David was denied the privilege because he was a warrior and had shed blood. The Chronicler nevertheless states that David handed on to his son Solomon a detailed plan for the building, together with gold, silver, precious stones for its decoration and also left him the Temple vessels.

SOLOMON'S TEMPLE

Under David's brilliant leadership, the united kingdom became a formidable power in the area with extensive boundaries, and the Hebrew nation reached the peak of its political and military strength. King Solomon (961–922 BC) fought no military campaigns and occupied no more territory. He consolidated David's empire and gave it forty years of peace and prosperity. Solomon enlarged and

A *Hassid* and his grandson (left), and a young Greek-Orthodox monk (below), against the hallowed stones of the Old City. Right, a bazaar alley in the Old City under a light fall of snow

The vaulted bazaars and market alleys of the Old City have long been an attraction for local and overseas visitors alike, and the daily scene is colorful, crowded, noisy. In earlier times, each product had its own market area. The alley, left, running off David Street, is the very one described by a 13th century pilgrim as "a covered street, vaulted over, called the Street of Herbs, where they sell all the herbs, and all the fruits of the city, and spices . . . At the top of this street is a place where they sell fish. And behind . . . is a large place where cheese, chickens, and eggs are sold. On the right hand of this are the shops of the gold-workers." In another street "they sell stuffs", and then "you come to Butchers' Place, where they sell the meat of the town". Today, while some alleys specialize in a single product, the main bazaar streets offer varied wares, and one can haggle over a hand-embroidered gown next door to a kiosk selling oriental sweetmeats adjoining a store displaying trinkets of copper, silver and gold.

The side-alleys are less crowded, and there is room to stroll and room to sit and sip Turkish coffee and puff at the *narghileh,* drawing the tobacco smoke through a bubble-glass of rose-water. Several times a day, fresh *pitta,* flat Arab bread, is brought from the bakery to the bazaar cafes (right).

embellished Jerusalem, divided the realm into twelve administrative districts, developed diplomatic and commercial ties with neighboring countries, and built a chain of fortresses at strategic points to protect the trade routes.

The crowning achievement of Solomon's reign was the Temple. It took seven years to build, and although relatively small, it became celebrated throughout the Near East for its splendor. The building was dedicated in the eleventh year of Solomon's reign. The Bible describes the ceremonial procession of priests who carried the Ark from David's tent to the new sanctuary, that was filled with the glory of the Lord in the form of a cloud. Solomon encouraged the three pilgrimage festivals to the Temple: Passover *(Pesach),* The Feast of Weeks *(Shavuot)* and the Feast of Booths *(Succot).* On these festive occasions Jerusalem was crowded with out-of-town pilgrims.

Running off the main bazaar are stepped alleyways (left) leading to the dwellings of the market people, and these, too, are drawn into the world of commerce. The storekeeper (right) waits, relaxed and patient—until a passer-by shows interest, and then comes the sport of haggling, enjoyed—or suffered—by both buyer and seller.

Part of the traditional route of the Via Dolorosa, from the Praetorium, where Jesus was sentenced, to Calvary, where he was crucified, lies through the bazaar area (right). The path of His progress is now marked by the Fourteen Stations of the Cross, identified by a church, a chapel, a piece of column, or just a sign. The first two Stations are placed in the Antonia fortress, which had been built by Herod at the northwest corner of the Temple compound. This is based on the belief that the Antonia was the Praetorium. The next seven Stations are placed along the route, and the last five in the Church of the Holy Sepulchre. Below, the Fifth Station, where the Cross was laid upon Simon of Cyrene.

Pilgrims retrace the footsteps of Jesus, bearing the cross and pausing at the Stations with a prayer (left). The tradition of the Stations, the events they mark and their locations, is comparatively recent. It was developed only during the Ottoman period. There were faint beginnings at the end of the 13th century when pilgrims would be led along the "Way of the Cross"; but the first records of fourteen stations, not necessarily the ones familiar to us, appear only in the latter half of the 16th century. Not until the middle of the 19th century were the subjects and sites standardized into the Fourteen Stations commemorated today. Below, a pilgrim makes his way through the Judean hills to Jerusalem.

Below the Temple, Solomon built an elaborate palace complex which took another thirteen years to complete.

David and Solomon created a fusion between Jerusalem as the capital of the kingdom, the Temple as the central sanctuary of the nation and the Davidic dynasty, ruling under divine warrant. However, the unity of the realm shaped by these two outstanding monarchs was shortlived.

THE DIVIDED MONARCHY

In the later years of Solomon's reign discontent simmered under the surface, due to the heavy taxes and the forced labor exacted for the extensive building programs in Jerusalem, and the chariot cities and other fortifications elsewhere in the country. The resentment was strongest among the northern tribes of Israel, that had not become fully reconciled to the dominant position of Judah, from which the royal house was drawn. Solomon's son and

The annual Catholic procession on Palm Sunday, the Sunday before Easter, commemorating Jesus' triumphal entry into Jerusalem. In this picture, the congregants have just entered the Old City through the Lions' Gate, having started from the Mount of Olives and crossed the Kidron Valley, and are about to end their procession in the courtyard of the Crusader Church of St. Anne.

The completion of a new Torah scroll is always a joyful occasion, and the donor (left foreground), accompanied by his family and friends, is here seen carrying one, wrapped in embroidered velvet, through the streets of Jerusalem, from the study of the scribe to the synagogue. A Torah scroll is handwritten on parchment, a meticulous process entrusted only to skilled, pious and learned scribes.

The chapels and altars (below) inside the Church of the Holy Sepulchre mark the traditional location of Calvary, site of the Crucifixion. The chapel at the extreme left belongs to the Greek Orthodox Church, the one at the right to the Latin Church. The robed prelates (right) belong to the Armenian Church. The Latin, Greek and Armenian Churches are the three Christian denominations with major rights in the Basilica of the Holy Sepulchre.

The ornate entrance to the Edicule (left) in the center of the rotunda of the Church of the Holy Sepulchre. The Edicule contains the marble-covered sepulchre where, traditionally, Jesus was laid to rest. It is the Fourteenth Station of the Cross. Three lamps illuminating pictures of the Resurrection above the entrance are owned respectively by the Latin, Greek and Armenian Churches. The Garden Tomb (below), on a hillock outside the city walls beyond Damascus Gate, regarded by some Protestants as being the authentic site of Calvary and the Holy Sepulchre.

successor Rehoboam (922–915 BC) lacked the sagacity and tact needed to hold the United Monarchy together. With his accession it split into two small and squabbling successor states, the southern kingdom of Judah that retained its capital at Jerusalem and the northern kingdom of Israel, with its capital eventually established at Samaria, northwest of Shechem (Nablus).

The Hebrew nation was situated between the mighty empires that rose and fell in the Nile Valley (Egypt) to the south, and the Euphrates-Tigris river basin of Mesopotamia to the north-east. David's empire had been carved out at a time when the external pressures were relatively dormant. But during the period of the divided monarchy a new threat developed to Israel, Judah and their neighbors, from the Assyrian cohorts pushing down from the north.

In 722 BC the kingdom of Israel, after two centuries of existence, was wiped out by the

Peaceful religious study in a synagogue inside the Old City (left), and in a convent garden on the Mount of Olives (right) overlooking the village of Siloam to the south of the Old City, the original site of Jerusalem in the time of David.

The western slope of the Mount of Olives. At its foot (fore-ground left) is the Garden of Gethsemane, and adjacent to it is the twelve-domed Basilica of the Agony, a new structure built on 4th century foundations and completed in 1924. It is also known as the Church of All Nations since many countries contributed to its erection. Above it, midway up the slope, is the Russian-Orthodox Church of St. Mary Magdalene. It was built by Czar Alexander III in 1888 in memory of his mother, and its gilded onion-shaped cupolas are stylized 17th century Russian architecture. Part of the ancient Jewish cemetery may be seen (upper right), restored since the re-unification of Jerusalem after its desecration during the nineteen year Jordanian occupation from 1948 to 1967. Above it, on the ridge, is the new Inter-Continental Hotel, built during Jordanian rule over the strong protestations of Israel.

invading Assyrian army of Shalmaneser III. Most of its inhabitants were carried off into captivity, and became known as the "ten lost tribes". The kingdom of Judah continued to survive for less than a century and a half—most of the time as a small vassal state paying tribute to the Assyrian rulers.

The king in Jerusalem after the fall of Samaria was the devout and able Hezekiah. His first task was to revive the purity of the ancestral faith by restoring the Temple and closing down the "high places", the local shrines in which pagan rites had become rife. He re-organized the administration and defenses of the kingdom and repaired the broken-down walls of Jerusalem. His most remark-able project was to provide the city with an adequate and protected water-supply, the key to survival in any prolonged siege. The spring of Gihon was connected with a reservoir, the Pool of Siloam, inside the city walls by a six-hundred yard tunnel excavated through

The view (below) of the eastern wall of the Temple Mount from the portals of the Basilica of the Agony. Right, the "Pillar of Absalom" in the Kidron Valley, one of several monuments sculptured out of the rock. Long thought to be the 10th century BC tomb of David's rebellious son, it belongs to the Hasmonean period, and the cluster of monuments in this area mark the burial places of distinguished Jews from the 2nd and 1st centuries BC.

King Hezekiah's tunnel, part of the remarkable water-diversion project recorded in the Bible, carried out at the end of the 8th century BC and still in use. Faced with the threat of siege by Assyrian emperor Sennacherib, and the need to ensure Jerusalem's water supply, Hezekiah "made a pool, and a conduit, and brought water into the city" (2 Kings, 20:20). He "also stopped the upper watercourse of Gihon, and brought it straight down to the west side of the City of David" (2 Chronicles, 23:30). What king Hezekiah did was to seal off the cave of the Gihon spring (left), which lay outside the city walls, and cut a 600 yard tunnel which brought the Gihon waters by gravity flow under the wall and into the city to the reservoir or pool of Siloam (overleaf).

solid rock. An inscription discovered on the wall of the tunnel ninety years ago indicates that the engineers had started the digging from both ends and met in the middle. It still carries water today, as it did when king Hezekiah "made a pool, and a conduit, and brought water into the city" (2 Kings 20:20). Hezekiah's adviser was the greatest of the Hebrew prophets, Isaiah. When the emissaries of the Assyrian ruler Sennacherib demanded the surrender of Jerusalem, Isaiah encouraged the king to defy the threat of destruction, and assured him that the Lord would "defend the city to save it, for my sake and for the sake of my servant David" (2 Kings 19:34).

The Assyrian army withdrew and the city was saved.

THE DESTRUCTION OF JERUSALEM

There was a cry of joy throughout the Near East when the might of Assyria was crushed by the revived power of Babylonia, and the capital city of Nineveh was sacked in 612 BC. But the relief was premature. Soon the Babylonian armies were marching west and south, and an Egyptian force sent to block their advance was routed. Babylon was now the master of the Near East. In 602 BC Jerusalem surrendered. The young king and many leading citizens were taken into captivity and a puppet ruler installed on the throne. In spite of grim warnings from the prophet Jeremiah, an abortive rebellion was launched in 587 BC against the new overlords. This time retribution was merciless. Jerusalem was sacked, the Temple destroyed, and a great part of the inhabitants rounded up and carried off to Babylonia. It seemed as though Jewish statehood had been terminated for all time.

THE EXILE AND THE RETURN

The pain and longing of the exiles found

59

The ancient pool of Siloam (left), the reservoir-terminal of king Hezekiah's tunnel, used to this day by the villagers of Siloam. Below, the newly built Church of St. Lazarus in Bethany, constructed on the site of a Byzantine church commemorating the restoration to life of Lazarus, the friend of Jesus, as recounted in the Gospel of St. John. Bethany, a village on the eastern slope of the Mount of Olives, was the home of Lazarus and his two sisters, Mary and Martha.

Solemn blasts of the *shofar* (ram's horn) echoing across the Valley of Hinnom from the slopes of Mount Zion (left) on Rosh Hashanah, the festival of the Jewish New Year. Mount Zion is the hill which skirts the southwestern corner of the Old City. It is held by some to be the traditional burial place of king David, and devout visitors light candles in this chamber (right), known as the tomb of David.

poignant expression in the words of Psalm 137:

> *"By the waters of Babylon,*
> *there we sat down and wept,*
> *when we remembered Zion. . . .*
> *How shall we sing the Lord's song*
> *in a foreign land?*
> *If I forget you, O Jerusalem,*
> *let my right hand wither!*
> *Let my tongue cleave*
>   *to the roof of my mouth,*
> *if I do not remember you,*
> *if I do not set Jerusalem*
> *above my highest joy!"*

But gradually the exiles settled down to a diaspora existence. They were sustained by the hope of a return held out by two major prophets. One was Ezekiel, the master of bizarre visions. The other was the unknown prophet simply called by biblical scholars the "Second Isaiah", to whom they attribute the latter part of the Book of Isaiah. This

The church and monastery of the Dormition Abbey on Mount Zion, its cupola and towering belfry familiar Jerusalem landmarks. According to Christian tradition, this is where Mary died, and the name of the abbey, Dormitio Sanctae Mariae, means the Sleep of St. Mary. It is a new building, erected in this century on the site of a Byzantine basilica. At the edge of the decorated floor beneath the dome of the circular church are steps which lead down to a crypt, and in the center is a reclining statue of Mary on her deathbed. In the foreground is the biblical Valley of Hinnom.

part of the Book opens in Chapter 40 with the famous words:

"Comfort, comfort my people,
says your God.
Speak tenderly to Jerusalem,
and cry to her
that her warfare is ended,
that her iniquity is pardoned,
that she has received from the
Lord's hand
double for all her sins."

The return was not long deferred. A half century after the destruction of Jerusalem, the Babylonian empire was defeated by King Cyrus of Persia. The following year, in 538 BC, this benevolent ruler decreed that those Jews who wished to do so would be assisted to return to Jerusalem and rebuild their city and their Temple. An expedition was organized and set out under Sheshbazzar, a prince of the Judean royal house. Under his nephew Zerubbabel as governor, the Second Temple

The Coenaculum, the most venerated Christian site on Mount Zion. It is located in the same building as the tomb of David, and above it, on the second floor. This was held by Christian tradition to be the "upper room" mentioned in the New Testament where Jesus and his disciples celebrated the first night of the Jewish Festival of Passover, an event known ever since as the "Last Supper". The Coenaculum, which means refectory or dining-hall, was rebuilt in the Gothic style by Franciscan monks in the 14th century on the ruins of a 12th century Crusader church.

was slowly rebuilt, in spite of obstruction from local elements. When the court official Nehemiah became governor, the city walls were restored. Another large group of returnees arrived with Ezra the Scribe, who carried out religious reforms that had a profound impact on the later development of Judaism. The new Temple was a modest and unpretentious structure compared to that of Solomon, but it acquired the same mystical appeal for Jews everywhere, as the focus of faith, pilgrimage and hope of national redemption.

THE MACCABEES

In the year 332 BC Alexander the Great of Macedonia swept through the Near East on his way to the conquest of Persia and India. He died on this campaign and his empire was carved up among his leading generals. Two rival dynasties, the Seleucids in Syria and the Ptolemies in Egypt, contended for

The annual fair of arts and crafts held at the foot of Mount Zion. This area, which was a no-man's land during the nineteen years before the re-unification of Jerusalem in 1967, has now been developed as an art center, with studios and workshops for artists.

the possession of Judah, which lay in the borderland between them. At that time Hellenist (Greek) culture was pervading the whole region and setting for the affluent and educated classes fashions in manners, clothes, literature, games and forms of worship. The Seleucid ruler Antiochus IV (175–163 BC) tried to force Jewish conversion to Hellenist paganism and desecrated the Temple by introducing pagan deities and sacrifices. When officials and soldiers were sent out to impose similar rites in the rural areas, a revolt broke out in the village of Modi'in, led by the Hasmonian priest Mattathias and his five sons. They became known as the Maccabees.

What had started as a local revolt against religious coercion developed into a guerilla war with national independence as its aim. In 164 BC the Jewish resistance forces took Jerusalem and their military commander Judas Maccabeus purified and reconsecrated

69

The view northwestwards from Mount Zion of the new Jerusalem. The long low building across the center was erected at the instance of the Anglo-Jewish benefactor Sir Moses Montefiore in 1860 to house Jewish artisans. It was the first structure of a Jewish suburb to be built outside the Old City, and was called Mishkenot Sha'ananim, Hebrew for "dwellings of tranquillity". Montefiore also built the windmill just above it. The entire Mishkenot Sha'ananim area has been beautifully restored and landscaped since the 1967 Six Day War, and the original dwellings now serve as guest apartments for musicians, writers and artists of international renown. The tower, top left, belongs to the YMCA, and the stately building to its right is the noted King David Hotel.

the Temple—an event still celebrated by Jews in the annual Feast of Hanukkah.

The struggle continued until, with Roman backing, the Judean state regained its independence. It was ruled by the Hasmonean dynasty founded by the Maccabees. Jerusalem prospered, and its residential quarters spread over the Upper City to the west of the Temple Mount.

But the rising power of Rome proved an uncomfortable patron. In 63 BC the Roman general Pompey took advantage of the quarreling between Hasmonean factions to march into Judah from Damascus and take Jerusalem by assault. Judah, shrunken in territory, remained a Roman protectorate.

HEROD THE GREAT

In 37 BC the remnant of the Hasmonean dynasty was swept away when Herod was installed in Jerusalem as a Roman vassal king. Herod, who was actually a convert of Idumean origin, is one of the most controversial figures in Jewish history. He was devious and servile in his relations with his Roman masters, and cruel and arbitrary towards his family and subjects. Yet he was an able and energetic ruler, and a magnificent master-builder. In the thirty-three years of his reign, he carried out a monumental construction program, including palaces, fortresses, temples, hippodromes and public baths. But none of these building operations was comparable in scale and splendor to the rebuilding of the Temple. In "The Antiquities of the Jews" the Jewish historian Flavius Josephus writes that Herod esteemed the project to be "... the most glorious of all his actions ... and that this would be sufficient for an everlasting memorial of him ...".

Two years were spent in the preparations, and a labor force of ten thousand workmen was assembled. The actual building was

Part of a scale model reconstruction of the city of Jerusalem as it looked in the 1st century, on permanent display in the garden of Jerusalem's Holyland Hotel. The work, which took several years and was completed in 1969, was carried out with meticulous accuracy under the direction of Hebrew university archaeologist Prof. Michael Avi-Yonah, and was based on a careful study of all the available contemporary sources. The towers in the picture are models of two of the three built by king Herod to protect his palace, the site of today's Citadel adjoining Jaffa Gate.

Archaeologists at work on the most dramatic excavations being carried out at the southwestern corner of the Temple compound under the direction of Prof. Binyamin Mazar of the Hebrew University. Started in 1968 after the re-unification of Jerusalem, the expedition has made remarkable discoveries, exposing remains of structures and artefacts from successive periods of antiquity right back to the period of the Second Temple in the first millennium BC. In the process, the scholars have also exposed several additional courses of the retaining wall (below) with its huge stone blocks built by Herod to support the Temple Compound. It is in fact an extension of the Western ("Wailing") Wall. The excavations, which are continuing, have already shed much new light on life in the capital in ages past.

A New Testament discussion in an Old City street (left),
and the elucidation of a point in the Talmud in a Jewish
seminary (below).

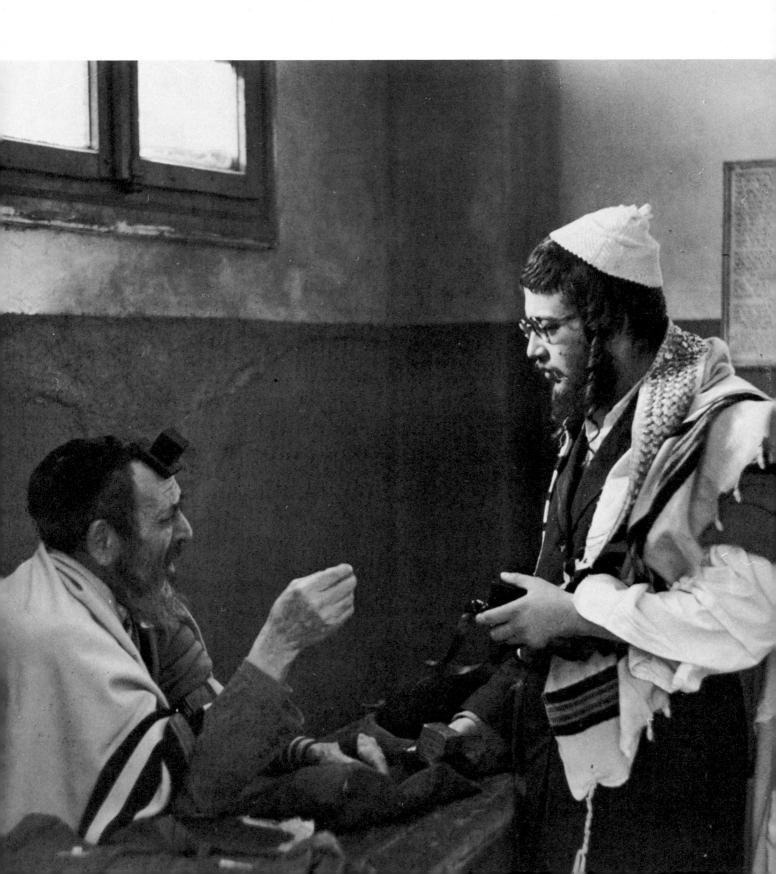

The mule at plough (right) within sight of the Old City may well envy the camel (left) on the top of the Mount of Olives whose only job is to offer the tourist a better view of the Temple Compound—and pose for pictures.

started in 20 BC, and only finally completed forty-six years later, after Herod's death. All that remains visible of it today is the massive retaining wall around the Temple Mount, part of which, the Western ("Wailing") Wall, is the most sacred of Jewish holy places.

THE DISASTER

After Herod's death the kingdom disintegrated, and was parcelled out by the Romans among his sons. Judah came directly under Roman procurators (governors) with their administrative seat at Caesarea, the port-city built by Herod. There was a brief interlude of autonomy with Herod's grandson Agrippa as king (40–44 AD), after which Judah reverted to the status of a sub-province of Roman Syria. The heavy taxes, the greed and arrogance of the procurators, and the presence of Roman troops in Judah, led to constant friction between the authorities and the local Jewish population. The simmering

Some of the older sections of Mea She'arim look much as they did in 1875 when this ultra-orthodox Jewish quarter was established outside the walls of the Old City. It attracted the pious from the European *stetl,* many of whom retained their former mode of life—even to wearing the same garb. Some of the children, too, still dress in these clothes.

The study of the Torah is the principal preoccupation of the orthodox Jews of Mea She'arim, from kindergarten to advanced Talmudic seminary *(yeshiva)*. Jews throughout the generations have followed the injunction uttered by Moses three thousand three hundred years ago in his celebrated valedictory address "Hear, O Israel": "... And these words, which I command thee this day, shall be in thine heart: And thou shalt teach them diligently unto thy children": (Deuteronomy 6:4–7).

discontent came to a head through heavy-handed interference with the Temple.

In 66 AD the Jewish revolt broke out and disorders spread through the country. Roman rule collapsed, and troops were rushed in from elsewhere. In 70 AD, after a long siege, the Roman legions under the command of Titus (later Emperor) breached the walls of Jerusalem and overwhelmed the exhausted and starving defenders, most of whom were massacred. The city was sacked and destroyed, and the Temple went up in flames. Its treasures were carried off in triumph to Rome. Three years later the Jewish zealots making a last stand in the rock fortress of Masada at the Dead Sea died by their own hand rather than be taken captive.

In 132 AD there was another Jewish rebellion, led by Bar Kochba, who succeeded in regaining independence, liberating Jerusalem and restoring it as the Jewish capital and religious center. But only for three years. In

The Jews of Mea She'arim adhere to the religious commandments with fervor and love. They select with scrupulous care (left) the most graceful palm-branch *(lulav)* and the choicest citron *(etrog)* to celebrate the Festival of Succot. And children learn from a tender age to bring gifts of wine and cake (below) to family and friends as part of the traditional celebration of the Feast of Purim, which marks the crushing of the anti-Jewish plot by the villainous Haman in ancient Persia more than two thousand years ago.

135 AD, freedom was savagely crushed by the Emperor Hadrian. He destroyed Jerusalem and even expunged its very name from the map. On its ruins he had a small Roman town constructed called Aelia Capitolina, and this was to be its name for the next two centuries. Jews were banned from entering their Holy City or even from approaching within sight of it.

But wherever they lived, whether in the Israel countryside or in their dispersion throughout the Roman empire, Jews clung to the memory of Jerusalem with a mystic fervor. It remained down the ages the focus of their faith and their dream of a return to independent nationhood. The liturgy of their prayers was filled with references to Zion, the Jerusalem hill that had become a symbol of national redemption.

THE RISE OF CHRISTIANITY

One of the harshest of the Roman procura-

Matza, the flat unleavened bread eaten on the Festival of Passover, is prepared in special bakeries (left) and under strict supervision in Mea She'arim to ensure its purity. It must be undefiled by contact with leavened bread. Pots and pans must be scoured and purified (below) before they can be used during Passover.

Mea She'arim bordered the demarcation line during the years when Jerusalem was a divided city, and there was no peaceful contact between the Arab and Jewish communities. Since 1967, Arabs are once again a familiar sight in the orthodox Jewish quarter (below). Every day seems to be laundry-day in the rear courts of the old and overcrowded but scrupulously clean buildings of the quarter.

The memorial chamber on Mount Zion for the millions of European Jews who perished at the hands of the Nazis. It holds urns containing ashes taken from the main sites of the Holocaust.

The price of Israel's renewed independence. The military cemetery on Mount Herzl (below). At prayer near the Western Wall (right).

tors in Judah was Pontius Pilate, who occupied the post from 26–37 AD, and was recalled to Rome to stand trial for his cruelty to the restive Samaritans. Among the many Jews he condemned and had crucified was a young preacher from Nazareth in the Galilee called Jesus (the Greek form of the Hebrew name Joshua). His death in Jerusalem attracted little attention at the time. But his small band of disciples grew into a new sect that broke away from Judaism and spread to other parts of the Roman empire, mainly through the evangelical zeal of one Jewish convert, Saul of Tarsus, who became known as St. Paul. In the fourth century AD, Constantine the Great made Christianity the state religion. He and his devout mother, the Empress Helena, erected beautiful churches and basilicas at the sites in Jerusalem and Bethlehem connected by tradition with the life of Jesus. The outstanding building was the splendid Church of the Holy Sepulchre.

Israel's annual Independence Day celebration begins with a solemn ceremony at the tomb of Theodor Herzl, father of modern Zionism.

Then comes the dancing in the streets, introduced by a procession of folk-groups moving to the traditional rhythms of their community dances.

Dancing, pageants and processions also mark the merry Feast of Purim, in celebration of the foiled threat of annihilation of the Jews of ancient Persia, with the beautiful Queen Esther (below) as the instrument of rescue.

For the next three centuries Jerusalem was a Christian city within the Byzantine empire, as the Eastern Roman empire came to be called, abounding in new churches, monasteries and hospices for Christian pilgrims. Jews were still not permitted to reside in it, though the ban on visits was relaxed on the ninth day of the Jewish month of Av, when Jews fasted—and still do—in mourning for the destruction of the Temple. The remarkable mosaic floor-map of the Holy Land discovered in a ruined church at Madeba in southern Jordan has a pictorial panel depicting Jerusalem towards the end of the sixth century, at the height of its Byzantine splendor.

Not long after, in 614 AD, the country was overrun by a Persian army and Jerusalem taken after a twenty day siege. Many of the Christian shrines and churches were devastated. The Persians were in turn defeated

The *Seder* service on the first night of Passover, celebrated in traditional style by a Bukharan Jewish family in Jerusalem. On this night, Jews throughout the world recite the Haggada, as they have done throughout the ages, with its account of the story of the Exodus of the Children of Israel from Egypt and their liberation from bondage, and they serve dishes symbolic of the dramatic events of that liberation. All are enjoined to feel at one with their forbears, as though they themselves were slaves who had just gained their freedom.

fifteen years later and the Holy Land reverted to Byzantine rule.

But the restored Byzantine regime was to last less than a decade. The new militant religion of Islam was surging out of the Arabian peninsula. Six years after the death in 632 AD of its founder, Mohammed, the Caliph Omar reached the gates of Jerusalem, after sweeping through Persia and Byzantium, and accepted the surrender of the city. More tolerant than previous conquerors, Omar left the Christian inhabitants unmolested, permitted the Jews to return and granted both faiths freedom of worship. A story is told that when Omar demanded to see the Temple area, he found it had become a garbage dump, and ordered the Byzantine patriarch to crawl through the filth on his hands and knees. Omar erected a wooden structure on the site as a temporary mosque. Strongly influenced by the Hebrew faith, Islam also developed a special interest in

At school in Jerusalem the young ones rehearse the *Seder* ceremony (left), symbolic of the history of Jewish suffering and the struggle for freedom. A scribe in Jerusalem (below) at work on a Torah scroll.

Jerusalem. Some early Moslems identified the Jewish Temple Mount in Jerusalem as the site of the "far distant place of worship" mentioned in the Koran from which Mohammed was transported to heaven in his vision. But the two holiest cities of Islam were Mecca, the prophet's native town, and Medina, the Arabian port-city where Mohammed preached and died.

It was a later caliph, Abd el-Malik, who, half a century after Omar, enhanced the status of Jerusalem as a holy city also to Moslems. He had a political motivation since Mecca and Medina were in the possession of a rival dynasty of caliphs. Moreover, he wanted a Moslem edifice that would outshine the great Christian basilica, the Church of the Holy Sepulchre.

On the Temple Mount Abd el-Malik erected the Dome of the Rock. The site chosen on the Mount was the flat outcrop of rock which had perhaps served as the altar of

Young and old, in organized or ad hoc groups, participants from all over Israel and from overseas join in the annual pilgrimage at Passover time. It takes the form of a three day march through the Judean hills to Jerusalem.

In the intermediate days of the seven-day Festival, the different communities in their traditional dress enjoy festive picnics in the parks of the capital.

Elderly artisans at their traditional crafts in Jerusalem. Left, clockwise: basket weaving; preparing the leather capsules of *teffilin* (phylacteries) which contain tiny scrolls with excerpts from the *Torah,* and are worn on the forehead and left arm during morning prayers; silver filigree work; fashioning the *shofar,* the traditional ram's horn used in Jewish ritual. Jerusalem, with its development plans, now beckons the younger craftsmen to more modern occupations (below).

Fine secular libraries and modern "monsters" with flaming tongues as chutes offer interest and fun for the Jerusalem young of today.

The International Youth
Bible Contest held in
Jerusalem's Convention
Center is one of the dramatic
highlights of Israel's
Independence Day
celebrations. The young
participants from abroad,
Christians as well as Jews,
never fail to astonish the
Israel public—themselves
steeped in the Bible—with
their answers. All are the
national "Bible Quiz"
champions of their countries,
and they show a remarkable
knowledge and under-
standing of the biblical
Books. The contest is
broadcast and televised
live, and no program is
followed with keener
excitement or suspense.

Solomon's Temple seventeen centuries earlier, and from which Mohammed was said to have ascended heavenwards. According to tradition, this was also the rock on which Abraham had offered the sacrifice of Isaac. The Dome of the Rock was completed in 691 AD. This octagonal shrine with its golden dome and its walls covered in brilliant tiles is one of the most glorious buildings of its kind in the world. Close to it, on the southern edge of the Temple platform, Malik's son, Caliph Waleed, erected a larger rectangular mosque with a silver dome over its center, called El-Aksa. The whole Temple platform was given the Arabic name it still bears, Haram esh-Sharif (Noble Sanctuary).

THE CRUSADER KINGDOM

The tide of Islam was halted in Europe at the Danube and in Spain, which had been largely occupied by the Moors, Moslem Arabs coming in from North Africa. At the end of the eleventh century AD, Christian Europe launched a counter-offensive. The Byzantine emperor in Constantinople had appealed to the West for help. Wandering preachers like Peter the Hermit stirred up religious fervor by descriptions of atrocities against Christians in Palestine and the desecration of their holy places.

In 1095 AD Pope Urban II proclaimed the First Crusade, with the aim of regaining the Holy Land from the Moslem infidels. Some of the knights who joined it were brave and pious men; others were drawn by the prospect of wealth and adventure. In their march across Europe the ranks of the Crusaders were swelled by a rabble of the landless and the lawless. Their path was marked by savage pogroms against the hapless local Jewish communities, with the burning of synagogues and looting of property.

In July 1099 the Crusader forces broke into Jerusalem and its Jewish and Moslem in-

Ranged along the ridge above the Monastery of the Cross are the white pavillions of the Israel Museum, built in 1965. It comprises art and antiquities wings, an open air sculpture garden, and the white-domed Shrine of the Book (top right) which has on display the seven complete parchment Dead Sea Scrolls and other ancient manuscripts discovered at archaeological excavations.

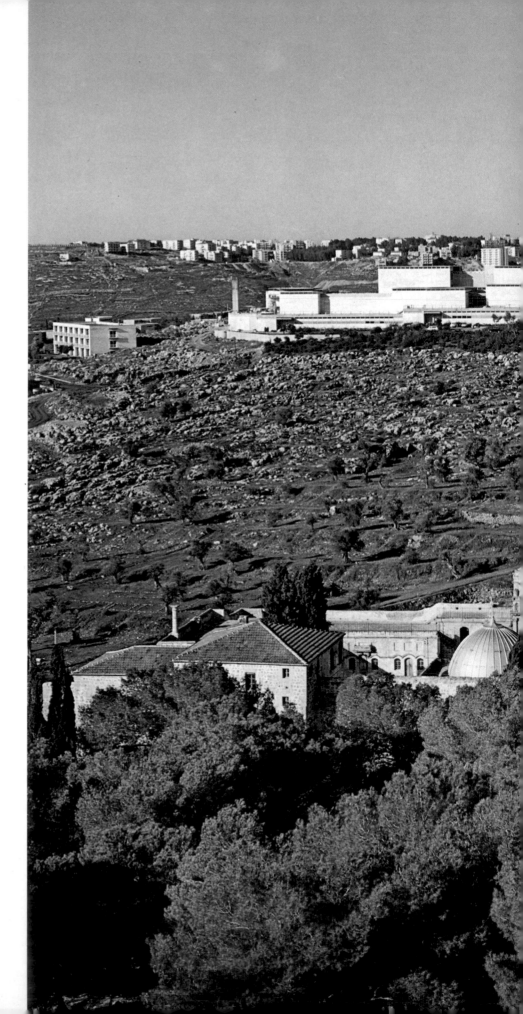

The terraced sculpture garden of the Israel Museum (left), designed and landscaped by sculptor-architect Isamu Noguchi. The centerpiece of the Shrine of the Book (below) is the 1st century Dead Sea Scroll of the prophet Isaiah, its 66 chapters displayed on a drum so that each word can be studied by the scholarly visitor.

The dome of the Shrine of the Book (below) with the floodlit building of the Knesset, Israel's parliament, in the background. The "eternal flame" (right) near the Knesset portal.

Jerusalem at full moon.

The entrance plaza to the Knesset. The sculptured iron gates (center right) are the work of the Israeli sculptor David Palombo. The huge bronze *menorah* (left), the emblem of the State of Israel, fashioned by the Anglo-Jewish sculptor Benno Elkan, is the gift of Britain's parliament to the parliament of Israel. On its reverse side, facing the Knesset, the *menorah* bears reliefs depicting outstanding figures and incidents in Jewish history.

habitants were butchered, the survivors being sold into slavery. Out of this bloodbath emerged the Latin Kingdom of Jerusalem, extending from the Negev desert in the south to the coast of Lebanon in the north. On Christmas day 1100, King Baldwin I was crowned in the Church of the Nativity at Bethlehem.

Moslems and Jews were banned from Crusader Jerusalem, that gradually filled up with members of religious orders and local Christian converts. New churches and religious institutions augmented the architecture of the city and the fine Church of St. Anne on the Via Dolorosa shows the building skill of the Crusaders. The Dome of the Rock was converted into a Christian church, named Templum Domini (Temple of the Lord), with the crescent on its dome replaced by a cross. The nearby El-Aksa mosque became the headquarters of the Knights Templar, one of the two knightly Orders

that were started in order to guard pilgrims and developed into powerful international bodies. The other was the Knights of St. John or the Hospitallers.

In 1187 the Crusader army was defeated near the Sea of Galilee, and Jerusalem occupied by the noble Moslem leader Saladin, who was of Kurdish origin. Like Omar, he was merciful to the vanquished. The Christian inhabitants were well treated and their shrines respected, except for the Dome of the Rock and other mosques that had been converted to churches which were now restored to Moslem use. Once more the Jews were allowed to live in Jerusalem.

By treaty arrangement there was a further interlude of Christian rule in Jerusalem for fifteen years until 1244. The city was then taken and sacked by Turkish mercenaries fighting for the Egyptian sultan. Christian control of the city would not return for seven centuries, until the British general Allenby

The Knesset in session (right). The Cabinet sits at the horse-shoe table facing the speaker, and the rest of the 120 members of parliament are ranged round them grouped according to political party. Above is the visitors' gallery.

The press box is in the foreground. Below, one of the tapestries specially designed by Marc Chagall which hang in the entrance hall of the Knesset. Its floor is adorned with mosaics, also the work of Chagall.

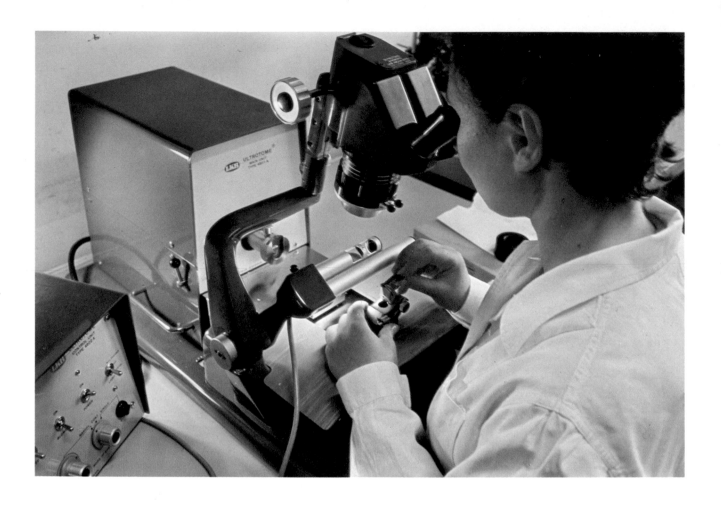

The colorful primitive and the antiseptic sophistication in modern Jerusalem. Above, a scientific laboratory at the Hebrew University. Below, right, the sheep market outside the Old City walls. Below, left, an itinerant street "butler" inclines his shoulder and skillfully pours drinks from his pitcher. Right, Jerusalem's Jaffa Road at rush hour.

Paris Square, in the center of western Jerusalem.

entered it in December 1917. The Latin (Crusader) Kingdom of Acre survived until 1291 when it fell to the Mamelukes, bringing to an end the Crusader chapter in the Holy Land.

The Mamelukes were originally Turkish and Circassian slaves and mercenary soldiers who seized power in Egypt and held it for over two and a half centuries (1250–1517 AD). They were ruthless fighters but great builders and patrons of the arts. In Jerusalem the city walls were rebuilt, and the Temple Mount area was adorned with fountains, minarets and tombs, and four handsome "madrasahs" (religious academies) constructed to make the city a center of Moslem learning.

THE OTTOMAN PERIOD

In the sixteenth century new invaders appeared from the east. They were the Ottoman Turks, a warlike Central Asian people converted to Islam. In 1453 they captured

129

The Yohanan Ben-Zakkai synagogue (below) at festival time. This is one of a complex of four handsome Sephardi synagogues in the Old City, the first of which was built in the 16th century by the learned and distinguished community of Spanish Jews who came to Jerusalem following the 1492 expulsion from Spain. In 1948, when the Old City came under Jordanian occupation, most of its synagogues and religious seminaries were destroyed. The four Yohanan Ben-Zakkai synagogues were spared destruction, but they

did not escape Jordanian vandalism. The interiors were completely gutted and filled with refuse, for they were used as a pen for goats and sheep. With the re-unification of the city in 1967, reconstruction was started, and after four years the synagogues were restored to their former glory.

The complete interior of this 17th century Italian synagogue (right) was brought to Jerusalem from the small town of Vittorio Veneto after its once flourishing Jewish community had disappeared. It is now housed in the Israel Museum.

The twelve stained glass windows by Marc Chagall in the synagogue of the Hadassah Medical Center, representing the predominant characteristics of the Twelve Tribes of Israel as recorded in the Bible.

Constantinople, and by the end of the century controlled Asia Minor and much of Eastern Europe. Syria and Egypt and the land between, including Jerusalem, fell to them in 1517. They were to remain masters of the region for the next four centuries.

Jerusalem was fortunate in that it attracted the personal interest of Suleiman the Magnificent who became the sultan in Constantinople in 1520. He carried out extensive renewal works in the city, rebuilding its walls and repairing and extending the aqueducts and cisterns that supplied its water. The existing walls and gates round the Old City of Jerusalem have remained intact since his time.

The initial Ottoman vigor spent itself and in the ensuing centuries the vast, ramshackle Turkish empire lapsed into corruption and inertia. Jerusalem also suffered from the general neglect. It sank into poverty and squalor. In the Jewish Quarter with its overcrowded dwellings and its twisting alleys life centered around the synagogues and centers of study, within reach of the Western Wall. The general population of the city declined, but the number of Jewish inhabitants grew through immigration. They were joined first by Jews from Spain, which expelled its Jewish communities in 1492, and then by a steady trickle from Russia and Poland.

The city started to revive in the nineteenth century. The growing interest in the Holy Land of the European powers created new religious institutions, consulates and commercial agencies. Christian pilgrimage increased and ancient churches were rebuilt. The "status quo" was reaffirmed regarding the rights of the various religious denominations in the Christian Holy Places, and the tradition of the Fourteen Stations of the Cross along the Via Dolorosa became established.

The Jewish community in Jerusalem con-

Three of the twelve stained glass windows by Marc Chagall (left). Below, the Hadassah Medical Center, built by the Women's Zionist Organization of America on a hill above Ein Karem on the outskirts of Jerusalem after access to the original Hadassah hospital on Mount Scopus was denied to Israel by the Jordanians in 1948. Following the Six Day War in 1967, the Hadassah buildings on Scopus are once again at the service of the sick.

Upper left, the latest International Book Fair in Jerusalem, a biennial spring event, which drew more than 600 publishers from 30 countries displaying 30,000 books. Upper right, an additional cultural amenity, the new Jerusalem Theatre and Concert Hall. Lower left, a new hotel to serve the ever growing numbers of overseas visitors to Jerusalem. Lower right, a not unusual altercation between driver and traffic police. (right), the Mahaneh Yehuda market in west Jerusalem.

Upper left, the open air amphitheater of the Hebrew University on Mount Scopus. For the nineteen years following the 1948 war, this mount remained an Israeli enclave within Jordan-occupied territory, but access to it was denied, except for a fortnightly convoy of Jewish police guards. A huge new campus was therefore constructed in west Jerusalem on Givat Ram (below), facing the Knesset and the Israel Museum. In addition to its faculty buildings, Givat Ram also boasts the impressive structure of the National Library—and its even more impressive contents (lower left). With the re-unification of Jerusalem in 1967, the amphitheater and the other buildings on Mount Scopus have been restored to university service and a vast new construction project started. Many new faculty buildings, research institutes and students' dormitories have been completed and are already in use, the two campuses of the Hebrew University serving the ever growing needs of higher education.

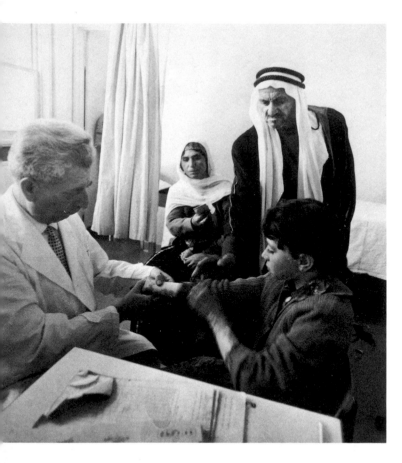

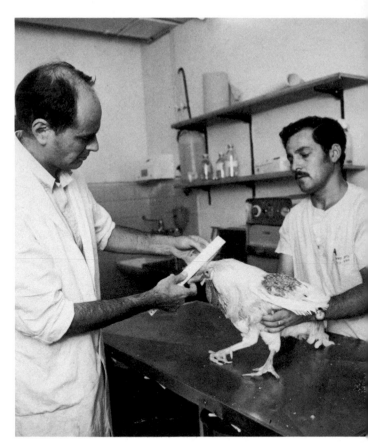

Upper left, an out-patient clinic in the Hadassah Medical Center. Upper right, a veterinary laboratory at the university. Lower left, a corner of the library. Lower right, the entrance to a faculty building.

tinued to grow, and from the middle of the nineteenth century to the present day the city has had a Jewish majority. In 1860 the pious Anglo-Jewish leader and philanthropist Sir Moses Montefiore, built a terrace of Jewish dwellings outside the walls of the Old City, facing Mount Zion. From this modest beginning grew the New City of Jerusalem. At the time, it was difficult to persuade families to leave the teeming safety of the Jewish Quarter for what seemed the isolated and insecure homes of Yemin Moshe, as the project was named after its benefactor.

In the late nineteenth century, the constant Jewish longing for Zion turned into an organized national liberation movement, Zionism. From about 1880 groups of young pioneers from Eastern Europe started setting up agricultural settlements in Turkish Palestine. In 1897 a Viennese journalist, Dr. Theodor Herzl, launched the World Zionist Organization. By the time Turkey lost possession of Palestine in World War I, the Zionist Movement had brought fresh life to that stagnant territory, and laid the foundation of a Jewish National Home that would evolve into the State of Israel.

THE BRITISH MANDATE

Under a League of Nations Mandate, incorporating the British Government's Balfour Declaration of 1917, Great Britain remained in control of Palestine and undertook to develop the National Home. In the thirty years of British rule, Jerusalem grew into a thriving modern city. It was the seat of the Palestine Administration, the headquarters of the Jewish national institutions and an important commercial center, benefiting from the economic progress in the country and the influx of Jewish settlers and capital. Middle-class suburbs spread over the western outskirts of the city. On Mount

The Kennedy Memorial in the Judean hills on the outskirts of Jerusalem, with its suggestion of a felled tree, in memory of the United States President who was cut down in his prime.

144

Types and scenes in Jerusalem.

Jerusalem boasts a unique Biblical Zoo, with a rich collection of animals mentioned in the Bible (below). Each cage bears the appropriate biblical reference. It is the hope of the Zoo director — and of the countless visitors — that Isaiah's verse "The wolf shall dwell with the lamb" will one day hang on a single cage.

Right, an olive tree in Jerusalem, gnarled by the centuries — still bearing fruit.

אֲרִי־נֹהֵם וְדֹב שׁוֹקֵק
מֹשֵׁל רָשָׁע עַל עַם־דָּל
משלי כ"ח ט"ו

AS A ROARING LION, AND A GREEDY BEAR
SO IS A WICKED RULER OVER
AN INDIGENT PEOPLE.
PROV. XXVIII 15

Scopus rose the Hebrew University, the only one in the country at that time, and the great modern Hadassah Hospital. The authorities helped to maintain the traditional beauty and character of the city by insisting that all buildings had to use, or at least be faced with, Jerusalem stone.

Unhappily the political conflict about the future of the country remained unresolved, and between the British, the Jews and the Arabs there developed "an unholy triangle in the Holy Land". In the face of Arab opposition, British support for the Jewish National Home waned. At the same time, the rise of Hitler and the flood of Jewish refugees fleeing from persecution in Nazi Germany, made the need of the National Home in Palestine more pressing and poignant. In 1939, during the appeasement period, the British Government issued a Palestine White Paper drastically restricting Jewish immigration and land settlement,

A burst of joy over the city
of Jerusalem on the anniversary
eve of Israel's Independence.

and projecting in Palestine an Arab State with a Jewish minority.

The Jews, and many Englishmen (including Winston Churchill), called the White Paper policy a betrayal of a trust—especially as there already existed a number of independent Arab States covering a vast area.

After World War Two the conflict became more bitter, and violence and military repression became common in Jerusalem, as elsewhere in the country. Jewish survivors of the Nazi death camps in Europe tried to break through the immigration ban and reach Palestine in small crowded boats, but most of these "illegals" were intercepted by the British Navy and interned. The most famous case was that of the immigrant ship "Exodus 1947", whose refugees were forced to return to Europe, escorted by British destroyers.

In Palestine, tension mounted daily as the British authorities faced a full-scale Jewish resistance movement. The Mandate had broken down.

THE STATE OF ISRAEL

At the end of 1947, the United Nations ruled that Palestine should be partitioned into independent Jewish and Arab states joined in an economic union, with the Jerusalem area remaining an international enclave. The compromise proposal was stillborn because the Arabs rejected it and resorted to force of arms. Britain terminated the Mandate and withdrew from the country. On 14 May, 1948 the independence of the State of Israel was proclaimed. The Arab armies immediately launched an invasion, and Israel fought and won the desperate War of Independence that followed. In Jerusalem, however, the Jordanian army succeeded in holding the eastern part of the city, which included the walled Old City, where the defenders of the Jewish Quarter were killed or taken prisoner.

The western new city remained in Israeli hands and was made the capital of the State. For the next nineteen years, Jerusalem was a divided city with a no-man's land running through its heart. No Jew was allowed to visit the Western Wall or other Jewish holy sites in Jordanian hands. Many of the old synagogues in the Jewish Quarter were destroyed and the ancient cemetery on the Mount of Olives was desecrated. The Hebrew University and the Hadassah Hospital remained in Israel hands but were cut off from the rest of Jewish Jerusalem.

In the Six Day War of June, 1967, this abnormal situation was dramatically rectified. Jordan entered the war against Israel together with Egypt and Syria. Jordanian artillery bombarded Jewish Jerusalem from the surrounding hills, and Jordanian troops moved forward in the city. In two days of fierce fighting, the Israel army recaptured the Old City, and the defeated Jordanian forces retreated from Jerusalem and the West Bank area, across the Jordan river.

Since 1967 the reunited city has witnessed a surge of energy and construction, and its growth has been more rapid and dramatic than at any time in its history. By 1976 it had become the most populous city in Israel. Under Israeli administration, Christian and Moslem holy places and religious interests have been protected and fostered, while for the first time in twenty centuries Jews have free and untrammelled access to their own sacred shrines. Jews everywhere in the world are filled with a deep pride and exultation that Jerusalem is once more the political capital and religious center of a sovereign Jewish state, as it first was in King David's time, three thousand years ago.

"Rejoice with Jerusalem and be glad for her all you who love her." (Isaia 66:10)